. Tokiwa-nazuna
. Bluets
. *Houstonia caerulea* A. Gray
inches high, by division.

J. Tanpopo
E. Dandelion
L. *Taraxacum platycarpum* Dahlst.
2 inches high, collected from the field.

start with the growing of herbaceous plants using inexpensive or locally procured plant materials. One of the best ways of all to begin is by attempting to dwarf wild flowers—dandelions, bluets, asters or any small flowered plants available in your vicinity. Besides helping you master the technical difficulties of miniature bonsai culture, these will give pleasure in themselves when they flower for you. Whenever you think that some of your native plants are suitable to grow as wee miniatures, take home some few plants and try them. Containers may be improvised, even shells gathered from the beach will serve. Make a hole in the bottom for drainage, fill them with soil, plant some young trees or flowers and see how they will behave and grow in their tiny new enclosure.

The Japanese have spent centuries developing the dwarfing of plants until it has achieved the status of an art. The word bonsai (pronounced bone-sigh) is from a combination of the Japanese written characters *bon*, meaning a shallow container, and *sai*, meaning a planting. A bonsai then is a miniature potted plant which can lay claim to be a true art form like a painting or a piece of sculpture when its symmetry creates a feeling of beauty. By following the principles of miniaturizing —restricting the growth by limiting the roots to

J. Otome-zakura
E. Fairy primrose
L. *Primula malacoides* Franch.
Ordinary pot plant, 6 inches high, from seedling. Miniature plant
grown as Bonsai, 2 inches high, from seedling.

the smallness of the container and by judicious pruning of the parts of the plant that are above ground—almost any plant can be dwarfed.

This book is dedicated to the smallest category of bonsai, descriptively called in Japanese, Mame bonsai or bean size bonsai. The limit of the smallest category is usually no more than two inches in height, though some of our examples are as tall as four inches, which overlaps into the next grouping called small bonsai, which are from two to six inches high. Medium bonsai are from six to twelve inches, and a large bonsai from twelve to twenty-four inches.

A rough division can also be made by grouping into three classes. The smallest, those that can be carried in their containers in the palm of the hand, the middle size, those which require two hands for carrying, and the largest, those which need two persons to move them safely.

The wee lovely things pictured appear delicate but they are not "hot house" plants, for they should be grown out-of-doors. They can, of course, be displayed from time to time in the living room, but they are in no sense to be treated as "house plants" and must be conditioned to spend most of their growing period outside.

J. Asagirisō
E. Mugwort relative
L. *Artemisia schmidtiana* Maxim.
5 years old, 3 inches high, from cutting.

6

A finished bonsai is the result of long years of endurance and patience in caring for it and training it to grow in a container. Unlike a plant living in a garden or growing wild, its daily watering cannot be neglected. Miniature bonsai are so small that they must be watered on the average of three times a day and in summer as much as five to seven times a day depending on the amount of heat and wind to which they may be subjected.

Also each watering involves wetting the plants three times: the first soaks only the surface soil, the second penetrates to the middle of the containers, and the third wets all the soil so that surplus water runs out the bottom holes. This incessant watering is the major drawback to miniature bonsai, an annoyance not only to the beginner but also to many connoisseurs. Beginners are likely to scant it and consequently their plants may suffer in the extreme and literally expire from lack of water. One of the great advantages of miniature bonsai, on the other hand, is the small amount of space they occupy. Provided that it is sunny or only lightly shaded, a shelf or area about three to seven feet is space enough to grow 100–200 plants. A collection can be so varied that there is no month without something in bloom or decorated with colorful seeds or fruit.

Mr. Zekō Nakamura watering his Bonsai collection.

SOURCES OF PLANTS

Like regular bonsai, miniatures can be grown from cuttings, or seeds, or can be collected as wild plants, and can be propagated by layering.

To make cuttings from a plant slice off small branches, using a sharp knife and making slanting cuts. Remove the tips of these slanting ends and insert the cuttings deeply at a slant into a suitable rooting medium which contains no fertilizer. Water copiously, set them aside in semi-shade, out of the wind and spray leaves from time to time. For most plants early spring when the buds are bursting is the best season to start cuttings.

Propagation from cuttings

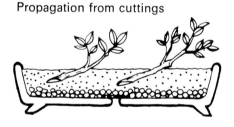

Insert them deeply at a slant into a suitable rooting medium with good drainage.

J. Miyasama-kaede
E. — *Trident maple*
L. *Acer buergerianum* Miq. var. *formosanum*
10 years old, 4 inches high, from cutting.

10

To grow miniature bonsai from seeds sow in early spring in the same kind of soil used for cuttings. Keep seedlings in flat for a year, occasionally giving them weak fertilizer and transplant them to single containers in the second year.

Of wild plants collected from their natural growing places, four- and five-year-old seedlings are best for training as miniatures. When a suitable small plant is found, dig it up carefully, trying not to damage any fibrous roots but removing the taproot. Leave some soil attached to the roots, wrap in moistened moss or newspaper and gently carry the plant home protected by a plastic bag. For the first year plant in a pot larger than the usual bonsai container. Although collecting promising specimens is most successful in the spring when the wild trees are beginning to sprout, they can also be acquired at other times of the year, especially if they are dug up with a fair amount of soil attached to the roots and then are given extra care at home for some little time.

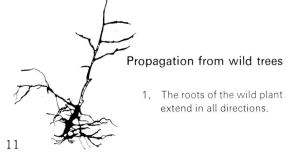

Propagation from wild trees

1. The roots of the wild plant extend in all directions.

J. Hinoki
E. Hinoki Cypress
L. *Chamaecyparis obtusa* Sieb. et Zucc.
20 years old, 5 inches high, from seedling.

12

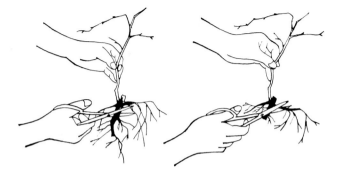

2. First, cut the taproot.

3. Leaving fine roots, prune long roots to fit the tree into the container.

4. Choose main branches with some personality, and cut the others away.

5. The pruned tree looks desolate, but it will make a good bonsai in a few years.

13

J. Ezo-murasaki-tsutsuji
E. Dahurian Rose Bay
L. *Rhododendron dauricum* L.
25 years old, 4 inches high, collected from the wild.

14

In air layering, a portion of a tree which is desirable to make into an independent bonsai is induced to root and is then cut from the parent branch. Early summer when the tree is growing most actively is the best time for this. Bark is removed over an area $2-2\frac{1}{2}$ times the diameter of the branch, and the wound is covered with well-moistened sphagnum moss or fine soil, which is then bound in place with a sheet of plastic, loosely fastened at the top for frequent watering. In a month and a half, new roots will have developed, and in two months the branch is ready to be cut off and planted separately.

Propagation by air layering

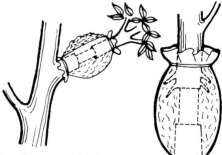

A portion of a tree which is desirable for making into an independent bonsai is induced to root and then removed.

J. Nishiki-matsu
E. Japanese Black Pine, Brocade strain
L. *Pinus Thunbergii* Parl. var. *corticosa*
20 years old, 3 inches high, by grafting.

16

SOILS

The kind of soil used for miniature bonsai is of great importance; yet it is also a highly individual matter. If authorities are consulted, no two authors seem to agree on soils and soil mixtures, nor is it probable that what works for one grower will automatically be the proper mixture for another. A soil expert advocates that a good soil mixture for bonsai should be made up of mineral and organic particles with no less than 50 percent "pore space" or empty spaces between the particles. These pore spaces are alternately occupied by water and a combination of gases.

It is customary in Japan to sift soils, usually comprised of clay granules, into as many as seven different sizes, then reconstituting the different sizes for varied plants. Some Americans, on the other hand, have been successful with little attention to this soil grading. They simply substitute coarse industrial sand and humus or other materials for the clay aggregates. Humus is the matter which holds the soil particles together in granules and occurs as an advanced step in the decay of organic material. Humus disappears rapidly from frequently cultivated soil which then loses its granular consistency. Therefore, soil collected from the root zone of a long established

J. Tachibanamodoki
E. Narrow-leaf Firethorn
L. *Pyracantha angustifolia* Schneid.
7 years old, 3 inches high, from cutting.

18

pasture or hay field is better than that from a cornfield or vegetable garden. When soil is collected it can be sieved into three or four grades according to the size of the particles and then exposed to the sun for several days until it is smooth and dry as sand. It may be sterilized before use, to destroy insects and disease producing organisms. Packaged so-called potting soil is not recommended, being extremely fine and already sifted the granular structure is missing.

The soil for bonsai must drain well. For perfect draining fine copper wire netting is placed over the drain hole in the bottom of the pot. This is covered with particles the size of grains of rice; finally the pot is filled with soil having finer particles about the size of grains of millet. A good mixture for both types of granules would be equal parts of red clay subsoil and fertilized topsoil. Well sieved granulated soils allow good drainage and never hold excess water. Even when water is given every thirty minutes, it runs through the hole immediately and so the soil is kept sweet and well aerated.

For the amateur it is sufficient to know that a fine loam soil provides a good growing medium for miniature bonsai. The beginner should try out various soils; there is no better teacher than experience.

J. Kuma-zasa
E. White-margined dwarf Bamboo
L. *Sasa Veitchii* Rehd.
10 years old, 3 inches high, by division.

20

CONTAINERS

The choice of containers is entirely one of individual taste and availability. The traditional ones are usually of glazed clay. For most plants shallowness is preferred to depth and all must provide a fair sized hole for drainage. The necessity for perfect drainage determines the survival chances of the bonsai, for few plants can remain alive if their roots are immersed in soggy soil, a condition referred to by horticulturists as "wet feet." The technical explanation is that all living cells, including those in the roots of plants, require oxygen to carry on their life processes. They are deprived of oxygen when the air does not circulate through the soil. If proper drainage exists, water soon drains to a lower level or out the drain hole and fresh air, including a full supply of oxygen, is drawn into the pore space as the water leaves. This exchange of "bad air" for good is necessary for healthy roots.

An assortment of containers. Match box gives size comparison. Zekō Nakamura holding Mame or miniature Bonsai.

POTTING

Before putting the plant into the pot, the root system should be examined and the older roots removed. When the plant is ready for the pot it must be studied to determine which is the best side to face the spectator. If a rectangular or elliptical container is used, the tree should be planted toward one end, the right or left according to the shape of the tree; in either case it should be placed at a point seven-tenths of the distance from one end just back of the middle. That is the best spot, not only from an aesthetic point of view, but for trimming, training and developing the plant.

The plant should be watered as soon as it is potted. For a week or more the pot should be kept in half-shade and foliage sprayed freely; and it should be placed in the sun half-a-day for four or five days, and after that exposed to the sun all day.

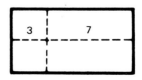

J. Yamazakura, Kyokuzan-zakura
E. Mountain Flowering-Cherry, "Kyokuzan"
L. *Prunus donarium* Sieb. var. *spontanea* Makino
13 years old, 6½ inches high, by layering.

24

Potting

1. Place a piece of wire mesh over drain hole.

2. Spread coarse granular soil.

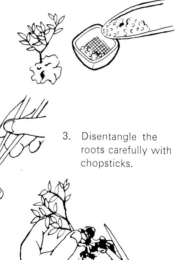

3. Disentangle the roots carefully with chopsticks.

4. Cut away unnecessary long roots.

J. Fukurin-asebi
E. White-margined Japanese Andromeda
L. *Pieris japonica* D. Don, *forma follis albo-marginalis* Maxim.
20 years old, 4½ inches high, from cutting.

26

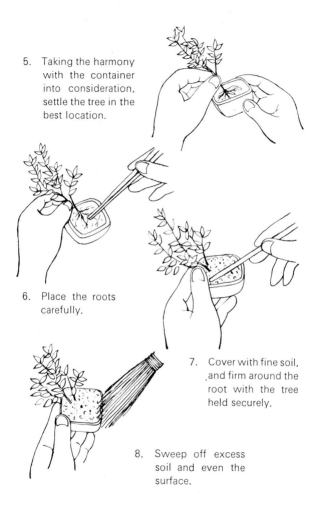

5. Taking the harmony with the container into consideration, settle the tree in the best location.

6. Place the roots carefully.

7. Cover with fine soil, and firm around the root with the tree held securely.

8. Sweep off excess soil and even the surface.

27

J. Fuji-zakura
E. Japanese Dwarf Cherry
L. *Prunus incisa* Thunb.
13 years old, 6 inches high from cutting.

TRAINING

The best style to follow is to copy the ordinary nature of the normal size plant. Bonsai should be miniatures, duplicates of the shape and characteristics of their originals and not grotesque dwarfs. A miniature bonsai of a large growing tree is trimmed like the mature shape of that kind of tree, though of course far smaller in size. Mame bonsai shrubs are like mature shrubs in shape and style, Mame bonsai herbaceous plants are like herbaceous clumps in miniature. Thus, Japanese Zelkova is broom shaped, cryptomeria is columnar, and pines are in the shapes characteristic of old specimens.

If the habit of a certain tree is to have a straight vertical trunk, the material selected for Mame bonsai of this tree should be young straight growing ones. If another species has in nature, thick roots spreading in all directions on the ground, the young tree selected should have its taproot cut off short so that it will have good development of roots on the surface in the future.

Although the trunk and a few main branches of miniature bonsai are sometimes shaped with wire, by far the largest part of their training consists of scissors training. These plants are too small for much wiring and it is better to be patient

J.　Goyō-matsu
E.　Japanese White Pine
L.　*Pinus parviflora* Sieb. et Thunb.
25 years old, 4 inches high, by grafting.

even though it takes more years—an average of ten—to produce a well trained bonsai. The scissors training can be very pleasurable as it brings close contact with the plant. In fact there are handling techniques which definitely contribute to the training results. For instance, a trunk can be thickened artificially by "exercising" it several times a week—that is, by holding it at the bottom with one hand while bending it from side to side with the other. The resulting separation of the bark from the woody part causes a kind of "inflammation" which leads to thickening. Be careful, however, too violent exercise can kill a tree. Another technique can be applied to the broom style Zelkova to hasten the desired shape, softly smooth upward the branches by hand whenever one has time.

Training

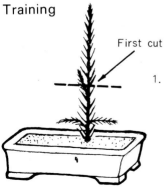

First cut

1. Young cryptomeria, showing where the leader is to be cut to keep the tree dwarfed.

J. Keyaki
E. Zelkova
L. *Zelkova serrata* Makino
10 years old, 4 inches high, from seedling.

32

New leader

2. New leader developing from small branch just below first cut.

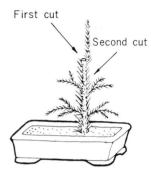

First cut

Second cut

3. A second cut has been made, on the new leader, and a third leader is developing. This procedure, repeated year after year, keeps the tree dwarf.

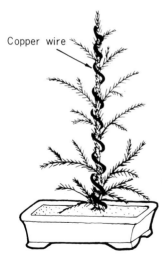

Copper wire

4. Young cryptomeria bonsai, wired to keep its trunk straight.

J. Hi-tō
E. Flowering Almond
L. *Prunus triloba* Lindl.
6 years old, 6 inches high, by grafting.

34

PRUNING

Young trees one to two inches tall are not ready to train with copper wire. Therefore a 1- or 2-year-old tree should be cut off at a dormant bud $\frac{3}{8}$ to $\frac{3}{4}$ inch from the base; after one or two years more it should be cut off an inch or so from the base. After such cutting back has been repeated for four or five years, the trunk gradually becomes interesting. Any tiny branches that are formed low should be encouraged until they become the longest, any that grow higher should be kept shorter by pinching back with the fingers while they are very young.

Special treatment is given to the shaping of flowering trees. The shoots of such trees and flower shrubs as well should be pinched about the middle of June. (That is the beginning of the rainy season in Japan, and the young shoots are hardening.) Only about two buds should be left on each shoot; from these buds new branches will grow in July and August. These branches are to remain untouched until autumn; in November they should be shortened, leaving some flower buds which have formed. Use a small pair of pruning shears. No special care is needed to induce plants to form flower buds if the plants are exposed to the sun all seasons.

J. Yae-shidomi
E. Maule's Quince, double-flowered form
L. *Chaenomeles Maulei* Schneid.
30 years old, 3 inches high, collected from the wild.

Pruning

Cut here

1. One-year-old seedling, ready for pruning to shape its trunk.

2. Two-year-old seedling.
   Note upright shoot removed, lateral branch allowed to grow.

Cut here

Cut here

3. Three-year-old tree, showing further training by pruning.

4. Four-year-old tree; trunk beginning to assume picturesque form.

J. Tsukushi-shakunage
E. Rhododendron sp.
L. *Rhododendron Metternichii* Sieb. et Zucc.
20 years old, 5 inches high, from seedling.

WIRING

In contrast to the development of an interesting shape some trees like cryptomeria must be encouraged to have straight trunks for maximum beauty of form. The trunk of the cryptomeria is repeatedly cut back year after year, to make it shorter and thicker, to have branches as low as possible, and to keep them healthy. If the trunk becomes bent or twisted, copper wire should be coiled spirally around it from the base up. The trunk can then be straightened, and the wire kept on until the trunk is fixed in the right shape and position. Copper wire burned in a fire of straw is easily managed and best for training purposes.

If one wishes to have a Mame bonsai with drooping branches like those of old trees, it may be done by coiling copper wire around the branches and bending them downward, as is done with ordinary bonsai. However, since Mame bonsai are tiny things, the wires may cause damage, so instead a weight may be hung on the branch to lower it. The procedure is as follows. The container is bound with light cord, somewhat like tying a parcel. The branches are lowered and held in the desired position by means of strings tied to them and fastened to the cord

J. Toshō
E. Needle Juniper
L. *Juniperus rigida* Sieb. et Zucc.
25 years old, 4½ high, collected from the wild.

40

around the container. The strings are left on for several months, until the position of the branches becomes fixed.

Wiring

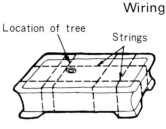

Tray showing the proper position for placing the plant, and strings to which branches may be tied.

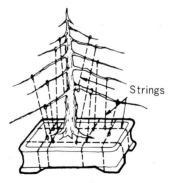

A tree properly placed in the tray, with its branches tied to the strings around the container to pull them down into a drooping position.

J. Goyō-matsu
E. Japanese White Pine
L. *Pinus parviflora* Sieb et Zucc.
30 years old, 3 inches high, collected from the wild.

FERTILIZING

Be very sparing with fertilizer. Miniature bonsai are so small that it is easy to over-fertilize and this is often fatal to them. In many cases they can utilize nutrients already in the soil and grow normally for a year or so without the addition of fertilizer. The object of fertilizing is not to make the bonsai grow but to maintain them in good health. Heavy fertilization programs will defeat the entire purpose of miniaturizing bonsai.

Liquid fertilizers, which are so highly diluted that the plants have no unpleasant oder when they are handled or brought indoors, are best. These liquids should be poured on only after watering. Beginning in late spring the addition of fertilizers is continued weekly through summer. During rainy periods it should be discontinued. In winter it may be applied occasionally. This schedule keeps the bonsai healthy at the same time that it helps in the dwarfing process. Growth is naturally vigorous in the early spring and during the rainy spells, and fertilizing them will simply overstimulate the plants. Over-fertilizing often causes the leaves to turn yellow or white, and to shrivel and die if it is severe enough.

When flowering trees and shrubs have matured sufficiently to bloom they require special feritiliz-

J. Issai-zakuro
E. Dwarf Pomegranate
L. *Punica granatum* L. var. *nana* Pers.
5 years old, 5 inches high, from seedling.

44

ing. When the flower buds appear, which will be at the normal season for each kind of plant, fertilizing should be stopped. For mature fruit bearing trees diluted liquid fertilizer should be resumed again about two months after the flowers are shed and then continued at intervals until autumn.

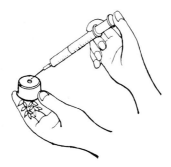

A Mame bonsai is sometimes so small that fertilizer must be applied by injection syringe through drain hole.

J. Tsuwabuki
E. Liguraria
L. *Liguraria tussilaginea* Makino
1 year old, 1¼ inches high, from
seedling.

J. Hime-ringo
E. Nagasaki Crab-Apple
L. *Malus micromalus* Makino
10 years old, 5 inches high,
by grafting.

46

REPOTTING

All plants become sick of their soil after a while, especially miniatures, which are growing in two or three tablespoons. So annual repotting, trimming one-third of the roots each time, is recommended. Even pines, which are transplanted and root-pruned about once every ten years when they are regular bonsai, require it every five years as miniatures. If repotted more frequently they grow too vigorously and break the balance of the trimmed branches and cause some of the lesser ones to become weak and die. Herbaceous plants are generally kept without repotting for five to ten years; in this way they look better and become daintier. Fruit trees are repotted annually also, but not in the spring, autumn is their transplanting time.

For the usual spring repotting the best time to begin is when the temperatures during the day average about 60 degrees. The procedure is the same as with regular bonsai, although with miniatures it is important to provide good drainage and to use screening over the bottom holes so that the soil will not be washed away.

To repot, the plant is taken out of the container and a large amount of soil is removed, very carefully, little by little, so as not to damage the

J. Goyō-matsu
E. Japanese White Pine
L. *Pinus parviflora* Sieb. et Zucc.
15 years old, 3 inches high, collected from the wild.

48

roots. Then the older shoots are cut off and shortened, and other roots and rootlets shortened slightly. The plants are replaced in the same containers filled with fresh soil of the same kind. They are then watered liberally.

Like a man just out of the hospital, the repotted bonsai need careful treatment. The leaves of broad-leaved trees should be cut in half to reduce demands on the newly trimmed root system. The foliage of all varieties should be syringed daily, and protection should be given from sun and wind for a week before the trees are gradually moved back in the sun.

Repotting

1. To remove plant, hold the pot with one hand and tap the wrist lightly with a fist of the other hand.

2. The tree together with soil will come out easily.

J. Yama-momiji, "De-shōjō"
E. Japanese Maple, "De-shōjō"
L. *Acer palmatum* L.
6 years old, 4 inches high, by layering.

50

3. Disentangle the roots with chopsticks.

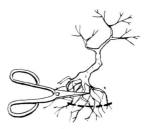

4. Trim long roots about by half with sharp scissors.

5. Place a piece of wire mesh over drain hole and mound coarse granular soil like a mountain.

6. Place the tree in the center and turn it round once or twice so that the soil may spread.

7. Settle the tree in the best location and fill with soil. Firm the soil with chopsticks.

8. Even the surface with an old paint brush.

51

J. Iwa-yanagi
E. Willow relative
L. *Salix vulpina* Anders.
10 years old, 3 inches high, collected from the wild.

9. Sprinkle plenty of water so that it may flow away from drain hole.

10. Keep the tree shaded for a few days, and then gradually expose to the sun, occasionally spraying with water.

DISINFECTION

Under normal conditions bonsai may need spraying with a disinfectant two or three times a month especially on the undersides of the leaves. Use an old tooth brush to wash the trunks with the chemical as insects, often invisible may be imbedded in the bark. There is a large choice of commercial sprays to choose from, just be careful to follow the directions. A homemade spray composed of cigarette butts steeped in water to which a little soap has been added makes an effective inexpensive mild spray to keep on hand.

J. Kan-boke
E. Flowering Quince
L. *Chaenomeles lagenaria* Koidz.
25 years old, 3 inches high, from cutting.

54

GENERAL CARE

As long as minatures are watered copiously, they will do best when kept in full sun, even at midday. Those grown in the shade tend to be delicate, and their flowers paler. For example, when a red-flowered plant is brought indoors for a week before it blooms, the flowers open pale pink and white. There are some fanciers, however, who say it is better to grow them indoors or under bamboo blinds or in half shade or in a cold frame. In areas where the winters have low temperatures which will cause the containers to break in the freezing process it is best to provide some protection either of the cold frame type or the plants may be brought into an unheated part of the house. Protection must also be thought of in the case of strong winds which could whip the small pots away. However, whenever feasible bonsai should be allowed to pass the whole winter weathering the elements, even occasionally being covered with snow and subject to frosts because in such cases the growth in spring is finer.

Since watering is so important it needs special emphasis. Generally in spring and fall water two or three times a day; in summer five times as a rule, but seven on windy days. If your area has winter winds and your plants are in a cold frame,

J. Tokonatsu
E. Daianthus sp.
L. *Daianthus superbus* L. var. *monticola* Makino
$2\frac{1}{2}$ inches high, collected from the wild.

56

water may be needed only once a day or every other day provided particular attention is given to any plants that may dry out more quickly than the rest. Since soil often freezes at night during midwinter water after ten in the morning and never in the evening.

If your tap water is highly chemicalized it may be irritating to the plants. If it is impossible to collect rainwater, the tap water may be put in a large jar and let stand awhile.

J. Tsuwabuki
E. Ligularia
L. *Ligularia tussilaginea* Makino
3 years old, 2 inches high, from seedling.
Leaf of normal size used as background.

Besides keeping the containers well supplied with water and adequate fertilizer judiciously applied, the plants must be well exposed to the sun and their growing shelf must be well ventilated.

The plants should be trained to their natural shapes. It is better to train and trim them with pruning shears than with wire. When new shoots begin to harden, they are cut back or pinched off, with two buds left at the base of each. Strong water sprouts should never be allowed to grow.

Repotting at the proper time should never be neglected. As the plants grow in small containers, it is essential to cut off the older roots and encourage new ones to grow. The soil must be well drained. The plants must have extra water for about ten days after repotting.

As the grower acquires experience, in one way or another he will cause the death of many plants; but this everyone must accept, since it is inevitable in the course of learning to grow bonsai. However, once one is familiar with the needs and reasonably careful, miniature bonsai will not die. They may live through three generations and be no taller than one and a quarter inches full grown.

It takes five to ten years to produce a Mame bonsai worthy of the name or fit to be admired. Indeed it is a trial of patience between man and

Mame or miniature Bonsai arranged on shelves.

tree. In the course of growing and training these miniatures for years, a great deal of pleasure and satisfaction should be experienced.

Mame bonsai will reflect all the changes of the four seasons—flowers in the spring, dark green foliage in the summer, picturesque colors in the autumn of crimson, yellow, and red and in winter solitude the still figures of the leafless deciduous trees.

The rules and suggestions given here may not work for you. As every collector's plants become accustomed to the environment he provides, they develop different requirements. One person's miniature bonsai, for example, may do very well when watered only twice a day, another's may die if not watered six times. When you have mastered the principles behind the rules, you will know what your plants need, and they will repay your care by growing their best, bearing flowers in the spring and fruit in the fall and so giving you joy in return.

This small book is from notes supplied by Zeko Nakamura based on his books in Japanese and his numerous articles translated into English which have appeared in many periodicals. The most important articles were included in the authoritative pamphlets of the Brooklyn Botanic Gardens; the first in the Autumn 1953, "Plants and Gardens" and the second in 1966, "A Handbook on Bonsai: Special Techniques."

Through the courtesy of Charles E. Tuttle Company Inc., their "Japanese Art of Miniature Trees and Landscape" by Yuji Yoshimura has been used as a general reference. Mr. Yoshimura, now practicing the art of Bonsai in Ossining New York, is Mr. Nakamura's long time friend. Fay Kramer, a member of Mr. Yoshimura's first Tokyo bonsai class for foreigners, compiled and edited the notes.

All pictures are of bonsai trained by Mr. Nakamura at his home in Tokyo.

Mr. Zeko Nakamura was born in 1900 in Saga Prefecture. He was a Zen Buddhist acolyte as a child and is now a famous comedian in movies and television. He recently authored two books in Japanese on his 40-years experience in growing small bonsai.

CONTENTS

Published by **SHUFUNOTOMO CO., LTD.**
2-9, Kanda Surugadai, Chiyoda-ku, Tokyo, Japan
© Zeko Nakamura, 1973
27th printing, 1992
Printed in Japan

ISBN4-07-975322-5

Distributed By
Charles E. Tuttle Co.

$ 5.95

定価650円
(本体631円)